HOW?'D THEY DO THAT?

in…

ANCIENT MESOPOTAMIA

Mitchell Lane

PUBLISHERS

P.O. Box 196

Hockessin, Delaware 19707

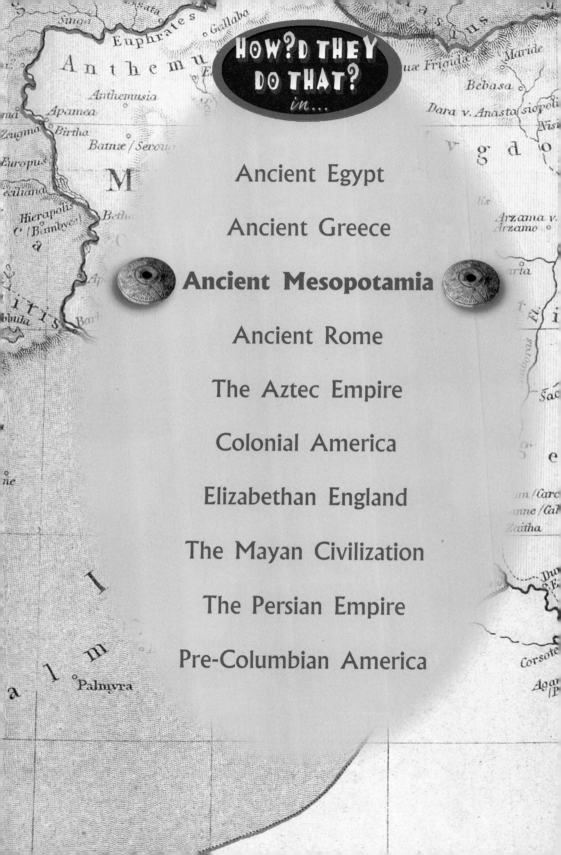

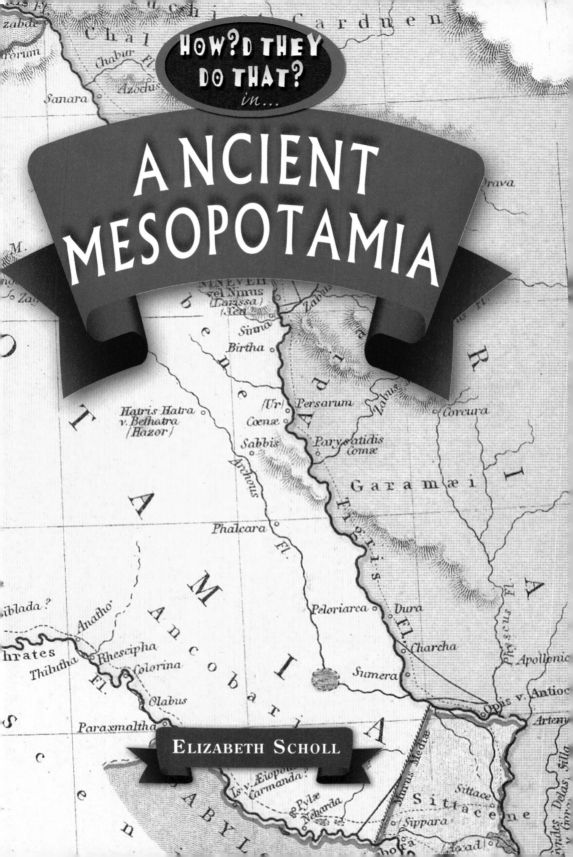

HOW?'D THEY DO THAT? in...

ANCIENT MESOPOTAMIA

ELIZABETH SCHOLL

Printing   1   2   3   4   5   6   7   8   9

Library of Congress Cataloging-in-Publication Data
Scholl, Elizabeth J.
  How'd they do that in Ancient Mesopotamia / by Elizabeth Scholl.
      p. cm. — (How'd they do that?)
  Includes bibliographical references and index.
  ISBN 978-1-58415-818-9 (library bound)
  1. Iraq—History—To 634—Juvenile literature. 2. Iraq—Civilization—To 634—
Juvenile literature. I. Title.
  DS71.S36 2009
  935–dc22
                                                                2009001299

PUBLISHER'S NOTE: This story is based on the author's extensive research, which she believes to be accurate. Documentation of such research is contained on page 60.
    To reflect current usage, we have chosen to use the secular era designations BCE ("before the common era") and CE ("of the common era") instead of the traditional designations BC ("before Christ") and AD (*anno Domini,* "in the year of the Lord").
    The internet sites referenced herein were active as of the publication date. Due to the fleeting nature of some web sites, we cannot guarantee they will all be active when you are reading this book.
                                                                PLB

CONTENTS

Kammani was not taking care of her younger brothers and sisters today, nor was she weaving cloth for her mother to sell at the marketplace. Kammani was sick, and she and her mother were going to the temple in the great city of Ur, the capital of Sumeria, where they would find the *asu,* or doctor. Kammani's mother hoped the *asu* would know what was causing her sickness, and what medicines would help Kammani get well again.

Kammani had developed a very bad cough. Sometimes she would start coughing and couldn't stop. She felt like she couldn't breathe, and her face kept turning red. When she wasn't coughing, her breathing sounded strange. She also felt hot and tired.

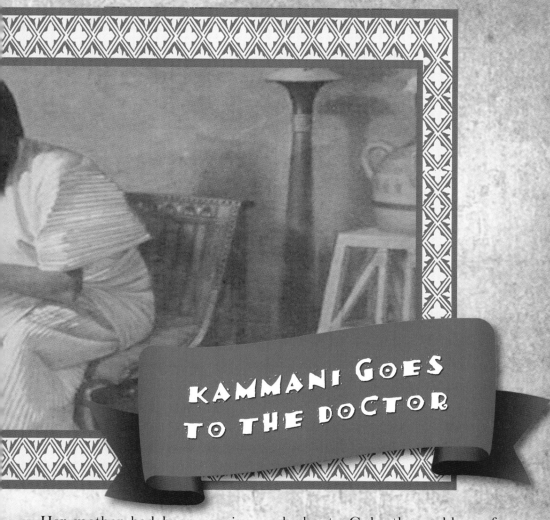

KAMMANI GOES TO THE DOCTOR

Her mother had been praying each day to Gula, the goddess of healing, in front of the family's shrine, but Kammani's condition did not improve. Kammani hoped the *asu* would give her some medicine to make her cough go away for good. She also hoped the medicine wouldn't taste too bad.

Kammani and her mother walked through their village toward the temple. Along the way, they stopped in the village square, and Kammani sat down. As was the custom, her mother told each person they met about Kammani's sickness. Each person, in turn, would tell them if he or she knew of such an illness. Perhaps the person had had the same symptoms, or knew someone who had. The person would offer whatever advice he or she could.

The Temple at Ur was built on a platform that was 150 by 200 feet, and was 75 feet high. The ziggurat, whose name means "high," represented a mountain. It was believed the gods visited the ziggurat when they came to earth, and priests and priestesses are thought to have climbed to the top to worship at shrines built there. Common people were not allowed inside the temple shrine room, so they gathered outside to pray.

The temple was built on a high platform. Although Kammani and her mother could see it from many parts of the city, it was a long walk away, especially in the hot sun. As they continued their journey, they could find no one with a solution to Kammani's cough.

Climbing the long and steep flight of stairs, they finally arrived at the temple entrance. Kammani looked around—the place was a flurry of activity. In the large shrine room, priests and priestesses were praying in front of an altar with a statue of the moon god Nanna. Some of them were placing items on the offering table on the other side of the room. It was mounded high with eggs, dates, figs, raisins, beer and

Frankincense

wine, and sacrificed animals, including ducks and other birds, sheep, wild boar, and even a bull. There were also piles of beads, gold, and jewelry. Frankincense was burning on the altar. They believed the smoke of this incense would carry people's prayers to heaven.

Kammani thought of the wealthier boys of the city, who were attending classes in another part of the temple called the Tablet House. There, they studied reading and writing from sunrise until sunset. Kammani knew of one boy who had been caned by his teacher because his writing was sloppy. For once, she was glad that girls did not attend school.

As they passed the large kitchens, Kammani could see a variety of foods being prepared. Jars of herbs and spices were in neat rows on shelves, and baskets of fruits, vegetables, grains, and meats were stacked on the floor. Women were busily grinding grain into flour, making bread, cutting vegetables, preparing meat, and making sure the fires were hot in the clay ovens.

Finally Kammani and her mother reached the special room in the temple where the asu treated sick people. Along the walls were shelves of jars that contained different types of medicines—dried leaves, powders made from ground seeds, pieces of tree bark, and mixtures made with

**Incense burner
5th century BCE**

plants and animal fat. There were also many clay tablets with cuneiform symbols on them, stacked on a bench. Kammani wished she could read the cuneiform writing.

When it was Kammani's turn to see the *asu*, he looked at her skin and checked her pulse and her urine. He asked if she had been behaving properly and obeying her parents. He asked whether she did or didn't do other things as well, trying to figure out if she had committed any sins. It was believed that many illnesses were caused by evil spirits, which could enter a person who behaved badly.

Since Kammani had been behaving properly, the *asu* felt there was no need to call the ashipu, who knew the spells for cleansing the body of evil spirits. The asu gave Kammani's mother some herbs, and told Kammani to take them mixed with milk and date honey. Then he gave her mother more herbs for mixing with animal fat to make a plaster, which she was instructed to smear on Kammani's chest.

After several days of following the *asu*'s prescriptions, Kammani was feeling better. Her cough began to subside. Soon she was able to resume her daily chores, taking care of her younger brothers and sisters and helping her mother grind grain, cook, and clean the house. In her spare time, Kammani worked at spinning thread and weaving cloth. One day she would make fine textiles, as her mother did, and sell them to the traders who would take them to the market at Kanish, two weeks' journey from their home.

An ivory or bone spindle whorl from 2000–3000 BCE. Spindle whorls provide evidence that women, and perhaps men, spent time spinning thread. Spinning was an occupation in Mesopotamia, and temples hired their own spinners. Spindle whorls were used to spin wool, linen, and later, cotton, which was imported from India.

10

FYInfo

Mesopotamian Medicine

Many ancient Mesopotamians believed that angry demons, gods, or other spirits caused people to get sick. Two types of healers treated ill people. One was the ashipu, who was sometimes referred to as a sorcerer. The ashipu would diagnose a person's ailment, then figure out which god or spirit was causing it. This diagnosis may have been done at the temple of Gula, the goddess of healing, a place where many medical texts were also kept. The ashipu used spells and charms to attempt to drive the demon from the person's body. Part of a spell used to ward off the demon Ti'u, who was believed to cause headaches, read:

An ancient Mesopotamian medical tablet

> The head disease roams in the wilderness, raging like the wind,
> Flaming like lightning, tearing along above and below,
> Crushing him who fears not his god like a reed.[1]

The asu was an herbalist, specializing in remedies made from plants. His treatments included methods such as washing and bandaging wounds, then applying a poultice—a mixture of herbs, grains, and plants wrapped in cloth. Mesopotamian texts also tell us that asus performed surgery, including procedures such as cutting the chest and scraping the skull to drain pus from an abscess.

From ancient clay tablets, we know that Mesopotamian doctors concocted most medicines from plants and trees. Leaves, seeds, or roots were used, and sometimes tree branches, bark, or gum. For a stomach problem, the asu might have mixed powdered ingredients that could be taken with beer, milk, or both, to help the patient swallow the medicine more easily. Another prescription was a salve made of powdered herbs and other ingredients mixed with oils or animal fats. The salve would be spread on the skin. Special soaps were made, using soda ash mixed with fat. Simply using the soap to rid the body of germs would often help a person heal. Rivers were also believed to have the power to carry away the evil forces that brought the illness. Patients would often stay in small huts that were built near rivers while they recovered.

Many stories from ancient Mesopotamia survive, such as the story of the Tower of Babel. As told in the Bible, the city of Babel (Babylon) tried to build a tower to the heavens. For this prideful act, God scattered the people and confused their languages. The tower has been associated with the temple to Marduk, and the story is similar to one from Sumer.

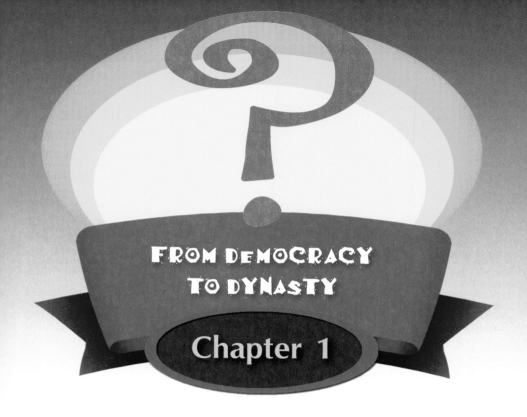

FROM DEMOCRACY TO DYNASTY

Chapter 1

Around 5000 BCE, agricultural, or farming, communities developed in the land that lies between the Tigris and the Euphrates rivers in Asia. Mesopotamia's name, given by the ancient Greeks, means "land between the rivers." The area that was ancient Mesopotamia makes up the modern-day countries of Iraq and Syria and part of Turkey.

Mesopotamia was hot, with temperatures often reaching 110 degrees Fahrenheit. Some areas were marshy, and others were dry, barren plains. Farming was possible only near the rivers, where there was fertile soil. The early farmers learned to use the water from the rivers by digging canals to irrigate their crops.

Mesopotamians grew grains such as barley and wheat; vegetables including onions, lettuce, carrots, and cucumbers; and fruits such as dates, figs, melons, and pears. They domesticated animals such as sheep, goats, and cows. These farming methods provided lots of food, so people no longer depended upon hunting and gathering.

With all the food farmers raised, not everyone had to farm to feed their families. People had time to learn new things. Mesopotamians were smart, and before long, they invented things we still use today.

Mesopotamians were the first people we know to use the wheel both for transportation—on carts and chariots—and as potter's wheels, to form clay into cups, bowls, and pots. They also learned how to make boats, which allowed them to travel along the rivers, carry goods, and trade with people in other areas. To keep records of what was traded, they developed the first system of writing. People began to specialize in various crafts and trades, such as pottery and metalworking. The first civilization had been born.

Once people began living and working together, they needed a way to make decisions about things that affected them and their communities, which were growing into cities. If canals needed to be dug, who would do the work? If someone did something wrong, who would determine a punishment? And who would decide if the community should go to war? What if an enemy threatened to attack? The people needed a government to help work out these problems.

GOVERNMENT

Around 4000 BCE in the area of southern Mesopotamia called Sumer, the first cities developed. These city-states had one central government that ruled the city and surrounding area. Uruk, the earliest known city, had 50,000 to 150,000 people, two temples, and many workshops, which produced such goods as pottery, fabric, clothing, and metalwork.

In the first cities, a group of elders (or other important members of a community) gathered to make important decisions for their city-state. In some ways, it was like a democracy. The earliest record of a congress meeting to discuss whether to go to war is found in *The Epic of Gilgamesh,* a story from about 2700 BCE. Gilgamesh was a heroic priest-king of Uruk (also known as Erech). The story tells how a city-state to the north, called Kish, threatened to attack unless the people of Uruk recognized Agga, the king of Kish, as their overlord. Two groups of decision makers—the elders and the warriors—met in Uruk. They, with the approval of their king, Gilgamesh of Kullab, would decide between war and peace. In the story, Gilgamesh proposes smiting, or attacking, the city of Kish:

The city of Uruk, built along the Euphrates River in southern Mesopotamia, was the site of the world's first monumental constructions. By 3200 BCE, it was the largest city in Mesopotamia, and perhaps even the world. Many historians believe Uruk is the same city that is called Erech in the Bible, said to be built by King Nimrod.

The lord Gilgamesh before the elders of his city
Put the matter, seeks out the word:
"Let us not submit to the house of Kish,
   let us smite it with weapons."

The convened assembly of the elders of his city
Answers Gilgamesh:
"Let us submit to the house of Kish,
   let us not smite it with weapons."

Mesopotamian weapons

Gilgamesh, the lord of Kullab,
Who performs heroic deeds for the goddess Inanna,
Took not the words of the elders of his city to heart.

A second time Gilgamesh, the lord of Kullab,
Before the fighting men of his city put the matter, seeks out
    the word:
"Do not submit to the house of Kish, let us smite it with
    weapons."

The convened assembly of the fighting men of his city
Answers Gilgamesh: "Do not submit to the house of Kish, let
    us smite it with weapons."[1]

Kings, who were also priests, ruled Mesopotamian city-states. A priest-king had a huge number of responsibilities: He led the military in war, was the head priest in charge of religious ceremonies, supervised trade with other areas, and judged any disputes that arose. Priest-kings were thought to be representatives of the gods, so by obeying the laws the king made, people believed they were doing what the gods wanted.

As their kingdoms grew, priest-kings required more people to help them rule. Many of these officials were also priests who were in charge of the king's lands. Because the king owned all the land in the kingdom, the people who lived and farmed on the land had to pay the king taxes. They could pay either in goods, such as grain, livestock, or other items they produced, or in services, which included working on construction projects, helping build canals, or farming on community land.

Fighting was common in Sumerian city-states, as rulers desired more land and power. In about 2300 BCE, the entire area of Sumer was con-

Sargon

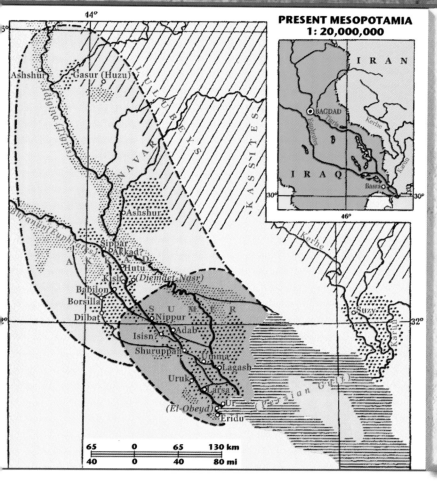

Mesopotamia lay between the Tigris and Euphrates rivers; Babylon lay to the south. The area covers the modern countries of Iraq, Syria, Jordan, Israel, and part of Turkey. Assyria is now Iran, and Babylon is now Kuwait and part of Iraq.

quered by Akkadians, who lived in the area of Mesopotamia north of Sumer. King Sargon of Akkad united all the city-states of Sumer into the Akkadian Empire. This empire lasted about 100 years, after which the city-states returned to independent rule.

During the 1700s BCE, Sumer was once again conquered and its city-states united. This time, it was the Babylonians who created an empire. Led by King Hammurabi, the empire eventually grew to encompass Sumer, as well as the lands to the northwest, reaching all the way to what is now the country of Turkey.

Powerful as the Babylonians were, their dynasty eventually fell as they were conquered by the Assyrians, who came from the northern

The Hanging Gardens of Babylon, considered one of the Seven Wonders of the World, were built by King Nebuchadnezzar II for his wife Amytis of Media, because she was homesick for the plants of her lush homeland. Described by Greek poets and historians as a terraced garden built with many levels, the hanging gardens were watered by an irrigation system. It is uncertain whether the Hanging Gardens of Babylon existed or not, as no archaeological remains have been discovered.

area of Mesopotamia. The Assyrians ruled until about 600 BCE, and they, too, were overthrown. The Chaldeans, led by King Nebuchadnezzar, rebuilt the city of Babylon, which had been destroyed by the Assyrians, and created the Neo-Babylonian Empire. This one lasted until 539 BCE, when Cyrus of Persia conquered it—and brought to a close the era of ancient Mesopotamia.

Cyrus of Persia

Hammurabi's Law Code

We have the best idea of actual laws and punishments in ancient Mesopotamia from the law code of King Hammurabi. Hammurabi, a great military leader, became king of Babylon around 1792 BCE. Under his rule, the Babylonian empire was expanded to include Assyria and northern Syria.

King Hammurabi believed that the gods chose him to rule over the people of Babylon, and to make laws for his people. He promised Babylon's chief god, Marduk, that he would create a system of laws by which the Babylonian people would live. The laws were written on an eight-foot-tall monument of black diorite stone, and it is believed, as it was the tradition of Mesopotamian kings, that many monuments were made and displayed in public places throughout the kingdom. The only known copy of Hammurabi's Code of Laws was discovered in 1901 by archaeologists in Iran. Historians think it was carried from Babylon to Iran, after Babylon was conquered. Today the Law Code of Hammurabi is on display in the Louvre, a museum in Paris.

Hammurabi

While Hammurabi's code was not the first written set of laws in Mesopotamia, it is the most complete. It covered all aspects of Babylonian society, from family life to crimes and punishment. Absolute respect for one's parents was reflected in the law: "If a son strike his father, his hands shall be hewn off."[2]

Criminal law was based on the concept of "an eye for an eye, a tooth for a tooth," meaning the punishment would equal the crime. King Hammurabi wrote, "If he break another man's bone, his bone shall be broken," and, "If a man put out the eye of another man, his eye shall be put out."[3]

Hammurabi's Code of Law

Hammurabi's code tells us that Mesopotamians followed strict rules about right and wrong behavior, and the consequences of breaking the law were severe.

Some reed homes, called mudhif, were built to be as elaborate as cathedrals. These grand structures were built for the sheiks, or tribe leaders. Inside, the mudhif had reed mats, wool rugs, and a hearth for cooking. There was a workshop area in the rear, and a barn for water buffalo.

HOME BETWEEN THE RIVERS

Chapter 2

In ancient Mesopotamia, homes were built from long grasses called reeds that grew in the marshes, or mud bricks made from clay found near the rivers. Stone and wood were not commonly used for home construction in Mesopotamia. Transporting stone from the mountains was difficult and costly. Trees were scarce, and the few that did grow, such as date palm trees, served to shade people from the hot sun. Despite their lack of natural resources for building, the Mesopotamians managed to create ways to construct homes, temples, and entire cities with what they had.

To build a reed house, men pulled reeds from the marshes and tied them in bundles. After gathering many bundles, they dug holes along the outline of the shape they wanted their house to be. To make the walls, a bundle of reeds was pushed into each hole, and then the hole was filled with dirt to hold the reeds firmly in place. The reed bundles on opposite sides were bent toward one another and tied together at the top to form an arch, which became the roof. For a doorway, a mat of woven reeds was hung over an opening. This technique of building reed houses is still used by the Ma'dan people, or Marsh Arabs, of southern Iraq.

Modern marsh Arabs pole their mashoof through a marsh in southern Iraq. Many modern Marsh Arabs have had to abandon their homes and traditional lifestyles in the marshes, because government irrigation projects have diverted water away from the marshes.

As settlements grew into cities, a more sophisticated method of home building developed. People began to make bricks out of clay mixed with straw. The clay was pressed into rectangular molds, then removed from the molds and either allowed to harden in the sun or hardened using fire. Oven-baked bricks were more desirable than sun-dried bricks, because they wouldn't crumble when they got wet. However, they were much more expensive to make. Fuel was needed to keep the fire going, and the workers who made them were specially trained.

Before a home could be built, the ground had to be made flat and level. To form walls, the bricks were stacked and plastered together with mud or a sticky, black tarlike substance called bitumen. The roof was constructed from palm tree logs, which were also plastered together

with the waterproof bitumen. Thick mud was packed onto the roof to make it sturdy enough for the family to sit or even sleep on. A special staircase was built on the outside of the house that led up to the roof.

Mud houses didn't last forever. When a house started to crumble too much to repair, the people would simply smash it down and build a new one on top of the mound of mud that was the old house. In time, the towns were built on hills, which were the remains of the old structures.

Houses were built around an open courtyard, where families ate and spent time when it was too hot inside. Sometimes the courtyards

Along the Euphrates River are large mounds or "tells," which are layers of mud-brick buildings, destroyed and then rebuilt on top of the debris. Archaeologists who have excavated tells like this one from Uruk have discovered that different levels provide evidence from different historical periods, from the time of agricultural villages to the time Uruk was a major city with a ziggurat to the god Anu.

were covered with palm leaves and flat planks of wood, if it was available, to shade them from the sun. Houses generally had no windows and thick walls, which helped to keep out the heat of the sun. They were whitewashed, which also helped to keep them cooler, as the white color reflected the sun's rays.

Mesopotamian furniture was simple. People sat on pillows or rugs on the floor, but there were also stools, chairs, and low tables. Beds were sometimes mats made from straw or reeds, with wool or goat hair laid on top. Wealthier people had beds with wooden frames, and mattresses stuffed with goat hair or wool. The Mesopotamians wove reed mats for the floors, and decorated the walls with wall hangings. Wealthy people had larger houses with more rooms, including a shrine room, servant or slave quarters, kitchens, bathrooms, a living room on the first floor, and bedrooms on the second floor.

What did people in ancient Mesopotamia do when they had to go to the bathroom? Though common people used the fields, the Mesopotamians invented something astoundingly modern, used by those who could afford it. By 2000 BCE, they had developed the world's first toilets and even sewers to carry the waste away. Wealthy homes and palaces had a type of toilet made from mud bricks with open seats. Sargon the Great of Assyria, in northern Mesopotamia, had several of these toilets in his palace. They had high seats similar to toilets we know, and actually connected to drains that led into a sewer. According to historian Samuel Noah Kramer:

> At Nuzi, a provincial Mesopotamian town, a luxury toilet was unearthed in the residential section of the Government House. The "seat" was made of two marble slabs. Low platforms beside the toilet were probably stands for water jars used for flushing.[1]

The common people washed themselves in the canals, but wealthier people used their bathrooms to wash with water and anoint themselves with sweet-smelling oils.

WHAT DID THEY EAT?

With fertile soil, river water, and innovative farming methods, Meso-potamians grew an abundant variety of foods. Barley was their staple grain, which was sometimes roasted, ground into flour to make bread, cooked into porridge, or brewed into beer—the Mesopotamians' favorite drink. Along with grains, farmers produced vegetables such as lettuce, squash, onions, garlic, lentils and other beans, cucumbers, radishes, beets, and sesame.

Lemon, fig, apricot, cherry, pear, and mulberry trees were planted alongside the rivers and canals. These smaller trees grew well because they received some shade from larger date palm trees. The date palm

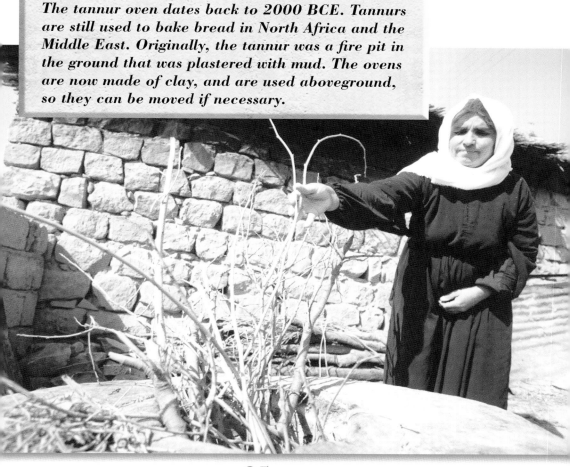

The tannur oven dates back to 2000 BCE. Tannurs are still used to bake bread in North Africa and the Middle East. Originally, the tannur was a fire pit in the ground that was plastered with mud. The ovens are now made of clay, and are used aboveground, so they can be moved if necessary.

was truly a multipurpose tree. Mesopotamians ate dates; they made date honey, date wine, and date vinegar from the fruit; they used date palm wood to make boats, carts, and wagons; and they used the leaves and fibers to make baskets, fishing nets, rope, and brooms.

The Mesopotamians raised animals such as cattle, pigs, sheep, goats, and a variety of birds. Besides meat, the animals provided eggs and milk, which the Mesopotamians used for making butter, cheese, and other dairy products.

Date palm tree

FYInfo

Mesopotamians had all the ingredients to create delicious dishes, but how did they prepare them? They wrote the earliest known cookbooks on clay tablets, and through the discovery of these ancient recipes, we know that at least royalty enjoyed fine cuisine prepared by a staff of chefs, headed by a *mubannu*, or embellisher—one who makes things beautiful; in this case, food.

Though they did not have modern ovens and stovetops where temperature could be adjusted, Mesopotamian cooks devised ways to control the heat of fires needed for cooking different foods in various ways. Dough cooked directly over a fire would likely burn before it turned into bread. The Mesopotamians found a solution to this problem. To make bread, they built a cylindrical clay oven called a *tinuru*. The tinuru was about three feet high and three feet long, and was placed into a pit dug in the ground. After the pit was heated by fire, flat loaves of bread were made by pressing dough against the inside wall of the oven. Today, this type of flatbread is still made in the Middle East and North Africa in a similar type of oven called a *tannur*. The *tinuru* was also used to steam foods: A pot of water was put into the oven while the food was cooking.

Soups and stews also cooked vegetables and meat without having to put them right into a fire. The recipe tablets describe broth made from water with herbs, spices, onions and garlic, and other vegetables. The cook then added meat and vegetables. Soups and stews were made thicker with milk, grains, and beer. A kid (baby goat) stew was made using this procedure:

> Sear (broil) the head, feat, and tail of the kid. Add the meat. Get water ready. Add fat, onion, samidu, leek, garlic, blood, soft cheese, all to be pounded together. Next an equivalent quantity of plain shuhutinnu [it is unknown what this ingredient is].[2]

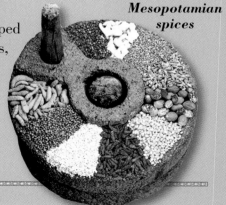

Mesopotamian spices

Many foods that are still eaten were first developed in Mesopotamia. People snacked on dried figs, dates, and raisins, and they used them in cooking. They smoked and salted meat and fish, candied fruits with honey, and dried beans and grains to use in various ways, such as in breads and stews.

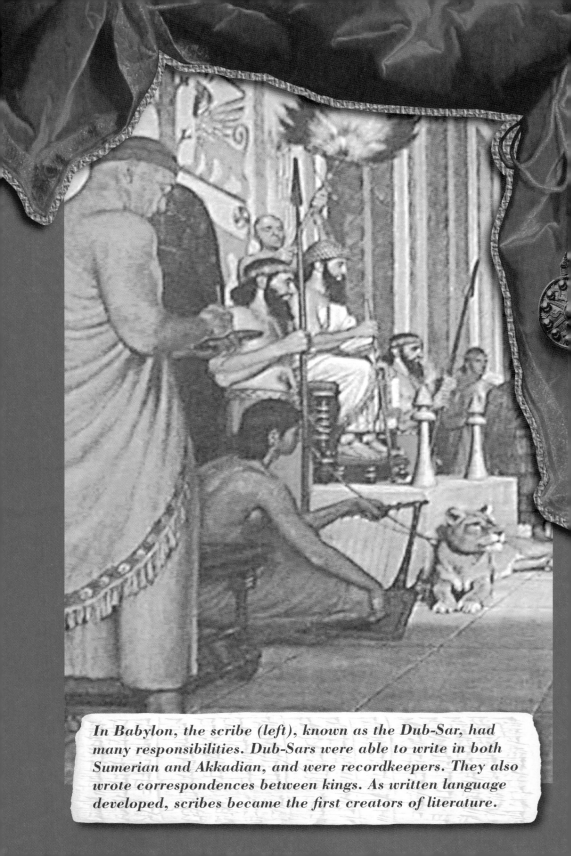

In Babylon, the scribe (left), known as the Dub-Sar, had many responsibilities. Dub-Sars were able to write in both Sumerian and Akkadian, and were recordkeepers. They also wrote correspondences between kings. As written language developed, scribes became the first creators of literature.

THE FIRST WRITERS

Chapter 3

Of the many things Mesopotamians invented, writing was one of their most important contributions. We can only guess how people lived before writing was invented and events recorded. The first writing was inscribed on moist clay tablets, using a stick called a stylus cut from a reed. Originally, large and small circles were used for numbers, and drawings called pictographs, such as a picture of grain or an animal, for words. This was a very complicated system, and scribes had to learn about twelve hundred symbols. Over time, the Mesopotamians developed simpler symbols for different things that were easier to write than a picture of the item itself. *Cow,* originally represented by a drawing of a cow's head, was simplified to a diamond shape, and later to a formation of wedges and lines. Writing formed using these wedges and lines was called cuneiform.

SCRIBE SCHOOLS
School wasn't a part of growing up for most Mesopotamian children, but when the Mesopotamians invented writing, they needed a way to train scribes. These professional writers recorded important documents

for people, from laws written down for kings to marriage contracts for common people. Scribes usually worked for the temple or palace.

Boys from upper-class families attended scribe schools, which were known as Tablet Houses or *edubbas*. While some girls of high rank learned how to read and write, they were probably taught at home, as girls did not attend school. The *edubba* was in the temple or at the home of the *ummia,* or school father.

In addition to writing, students studied math, botany, zoology, geography, religion, grammar, and language. They memorized and copied lists of things, such as names of trees, animals, countries and cities, and minerals. They also studied mathematical tables and problems.

The school day at the *edubba* was long and demanding. A clay tablet from about 2000 BCE describes the particularly rough school day of a young Sumerian boy. The day began at sunrise and continued until sunset.

In school the monitor in charge said to me, 'Why are you late?' Afraid and with pounding heart, I entered before my teacher and made a respectful curtsy. . . .

He had to take canings from the various members of the school staff for such indiscretions as talking, standing up, and walking out of the gate. Worst of all, the teacher said to him, "Your hand [copy] is not satisfactory," and caned him. This seems to have been too much for the lad, and he suggests to his father that it might be a good idea to invite the teacher home. . . . The father then wined and dined the teacher, "dressed him in a new garment, gave him a gift, put a ring on his hand." Warmed by this generosity, the teacher reassures the aspiring scribe in poetic words, which read in part: "Young man, because you did not neglect my word, did not forsake it, may you reach the pinnacle of the scribal art, may you achieve it completely. . . . Of your brothers may you be their leader, of your friends may you be their chief, may you rank the highest of the school-boys. . . . You have carried out well the school's activities, you have become a man of learning.[1]

LITERATURE

Long before written language, tales were passed down from one generation to the next by storytellers. As the first culture to invent writing, Mesopotamia also became the first culture to have literature, the art of the written word.

The Epic of Gilgamesh is the world's oldest surviving tale of a superhero. Gilgamesh was believed to have been a real king of the city-state of Uruk. According to the story, he is more than that—in fact, he was the greatest king on earth. We are told that Gilgamesh was two-thirds god and one-third human.

> My son, there lives in Uruk a certain Gilgamesh.
> There is no one stronger than he,
> he is as strong as the meteorite [word uncertain]
> of Anu.[2]

In the story, the people of Uruk feel Gilgamesh is too harsh a king. They say he prevents sons from helping their fathers, and daughters from helping their mothers.

The people complain about Gilgamesh to the gods, and the gods send a wildman named Enkidu to challenge him.

> His whole body was shaggy with hair,
> he had a full head of hair like a woman,
> his locks billowed in profusion like Ashnan.
> He knew neither people nor settled living,
> but wore a garment like Sumukan.
> He ate grasses with the gazelles,
> and jostled at the watering hole with the
> animals;
> as with animals, his thirst was slaked
> with (mere) water.[3]

Gilgamesh

Cuneiform tablets bearing pictographs and numbers. Many cuneiform tablets were stolen from excavation sites and sold to collectors. Researchers who study cuneiform writing on stone or clay slabs, called epigraphers, have had a difficult time deciphering the tablets. With the help of the Internet, epigraphers are now able to access images of cuneiform tablets online, to help them with their studies.

Before long, Enkidu meets a woman. As they fall in love, he loses his wildness and gains knowledge and understanding. He and Gilgamesh become friends, and they embark on several dangerous quests. They slay a demon and the "Bull of Heaven." When Enkidu is punished by the gods and dies, Gilgamesh is devastated. He then seeks immortality for himself. Although he does not become immortal, he does become a better, kinder king.

MATH

Have you ever wondered who came up with the idea that a minute is sixty seconds, or an hour is sixty minutes? It was the ancient Mesopotamians. In Sumer, people developed a counting system based on units of sixty, called the base-sixty, or sexagesimal (sek-suh-JEH-sih-mul), system. Our counting system, called the Arabic system, is a base-ten or decimal system.

The sexagesimal system developed by the Babylonians has continued to be used for thousands of years. The Babylonians created the 24-hour day, divided each hour into sixty minutes, and each minute into sixty seconds. Greek mathematician Ptolemy and other astronomers used the sexagesimal system to study the night sky.

An astrolabe. Babylonian astrolabe tablets consisted of three circles divided into twelve sections. Each of the thirty-six sections contained the names of constellations as well as numbers. It is thought that the numbers represented the months of the Babylonian calendar. Astrolabes are still used to determine the holder's position on Earth according to where the stars and planets are at a certain time.

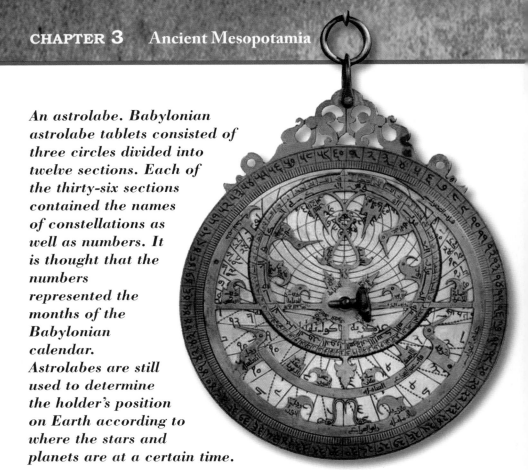

In Mesopotamia, mathematicians used both systems. The sexagesimal system was used for measuring weight. It was based on the talent—the average load that could be carried by a person or animal. A talent could be divided into 60 minas, and each mina could be divided into 60 shekels.

Place value was also created by the Mesopotamians. Just as the 5 in the number 256 means 5 tens, or 50, in our mathematical system, the placement of a Sumerian digit determined the digit's value.

Can you imagine math without zero? The Sumerians just left a blank space to represent zero in a number. That could get confusing if a person accidentally forgot to leave the space, or if someone didn't realize there was a space at all. Later, in Babylon, the Mesopotamians solved that problem by coming up with a symbol that represented nothing.

FYInfo

Enheduanna

Enheduanna, the first known author, lived in Mesopotamia from about 2285 to 2250 BCE. While her writings are not the earliest discovered, she was the first known author to sign her name to her work.

Enheduanna was the daughter of Sargon I, the king of the Assyrian Empire who united Sumer and Akkad. Enheduanna was an *en*, or high priestess, and resided at the temple of Nanna, the Sumerian god of the moon, in the city of Ur. While most girls in Mesopotamian times never learned how to read or write, Enheduanna probably learned how to read and write religious hymns as part of her training to become a high priestess.

In addition to writing poetry to honor the god Nanna, Enheduanna worshiped the goddess Inanna. She traveled to and united many communities in her father's empire by convincing them to worship the goddess. When Enheduanna was temporarily removed from her position as High Priestess, she wrote a poem to Inanna asking for help:

> How supreme you are over the great gods, the Anunna!
> The Anunna kiss the ground with their lips (in obeisance) to you.
> (But) my own sentence is not concluded, a hostile judgment appears
>   before my eyes.
> (My) hands are no longer folded on the ritual couch,
> I may no longer reveal the pronouncements of Ningal to man.
> Yet I am the brilliant high priestess of Nanna,
> Oh my queen beloved of
>   An, may your heart
>   take pity on me![4]

Inanna being worshiped by lesser goddesses

It is not known whether Inanna answered her prayers, but Enheduanna did regain her position.

The Mesopotamians made a variety of figures out of clay. These may have been used as fertility figures, which were charms created to help women during pregnancy and childbirth. Charms for fertility may also have been used in relation to the earth, to ensure that crops were successful.

FORM AND FUNCTION

Chapter 4

Beautiful art was created in ancient Mesopotamia, but we don't know any of the artists by name. During Mesopotamian times, artists were hired by kings, priests, or wealthy citizens to create lovely pieces that also always had a function, such as a decorated pot for storage or a musical instrument with elaborate metalwork. Unlike later artists, who usually worked independently or were hired only for specific jobs (such as painting a cathedral), in Mesopotamia, being an artist, craftsperson, or musician was a job, just as farming, hunting, and trading were.

POTTERY

Probably because clay was abundant near the rivers, pottery became one of the earliest art forms in Mesopotamia. Early potters learned that when clay was dried in the sun, it crumbled easily, but baking the clay at high temperatures in an oven called a kiln helped make it stronger.

It is believed that women were the earliest potters. They made pottery for the needs of the family, such as bowls and dishes for eating, and jugs for carrying water and storing food. As villages grew into cities, more people needed more pottery. Jobs in Mesopotamian society began to become more specialized, and women, who were also responsible for preparing food and caring for the children, could never be full-time potters. Pottery making became a man's trade. With the invention of the potter's wheel, men could produce many more pieces of pottery working all day than a woman could in her spare time.

The potter's wheel helped Mesopotamians make more sophisticated-looking pottery, and much more quickly than using the coil method of forming strips of clay and building them into the walls of a pot. The pottery was baked in dome-shaped kilns at about 900 degrees Fahrenheit. Glazes, made from powdered minerals such as quartz or iron oxide, made the pottery stronger and waterproof, and they also gave it a colorful finish. Black, brown, red, white, and orange were the most common colors for Mesopotamian pottery, and designs such as birds and animals were often etched into the surface of the clay.

CYLINDER SEALS

Of all the art forms that came from Mesopotamian times, the cylinder seal is the best known. Cylinder seals were tiny barrel-shaped objects, most often made of stone, engraved with a variety of images. Though they did not usually have words, these tiny engravings show us scenes of daily life, including farming and weaving, banquets with musicians and dancers, and warriors in combat. Some seals depict scenes from myths like *The Epic of Gilgamesh* or from religious stories, and include images of kings and gods. Various types of animals, birds, and insects were also included in pictures on cylinder seals. British archaeologist Sir Leonard Woolley writes:

> the fashion of the cylinder seals . . . the ritual banquet, with seated figures drinking through tubes, and scenes of Gilgamesh, or Gilgamesh and his friend Enkidu, in combat with lions or bulls. These two subjects are repeated with infinite variations and sometimes, in the case of the combat scenes, with a very forceful realism, and the cutting is extremely fine.[1]

Cylinder seals were rolled on the wet clay of an object to be marked. They were used as a way of signing one's work, as well as of identifying

Cylinder seals depicted animals as well as images of people engaged in a variety of activities, such as feasting and warfare. This cylinder seal, made of lapis lazuli, is carved with an image of two men drinking from a large pot, and a table of food behind them. Another part of the seal is engraved with a bird hovering between two horned animals.

things people owned. Like rubber stamps, they were used as official signatures to make documents legal. When they were used to seal packages, they could identify who manufactured or packed the contents. Cylinder seals were such important tools in Mesopotamian society, they continued to be used for three thousand years.

The art of cylinder seal cutting took four years of training under a master *burgul*, or seal maker. An apprentice would learn how to use a variety of copper and bronze tools to engrave the seals in such a way that the pictures would be raised when rolled on wet clay. A seal cutter had to keep in mind that whatever he carved would come out

in reverse on clay. This was especially important if cuneiform writing was carved into the seal, such as someone's name or occupation. The seal maker also used a tool called a borer to drill a hole through the cylinder. It was common for people to wear their cylinder seal on a string around their neck.

JEWELRY

In ancient Mesopotamia, jewelry was valued by men and women. It was commonly given as gifts, both among rulers and by common people for special occasions such as weddings and childbirth. Metal was not mined in Mesopotamia, so gold and silver were imported from neighboring lands such as Iran and Anatolia. Likewise, popular stones such as lapis lazuli and carnelian were obtained through trade with Afghanistan and India.

Necklaces, bracelets, rings, earrings, anklets, pins, and armlets worn on the upper arm were all fashionable in Mesopotamia. Hairpins and hair ribbons made from silver and gold were worn by wealthy women. Popular designs for jewelry were cone and spiral shapes, as well as the shapes of leaves and bunches of grapes. For identification, women and children wore rings with carved gems in them. Like cylinder seals, when the stone was pressed into clay, the carving in the ring signed the wearer's name.

People wore jewelry even after they died. Mesopotamians believed in an afterlife—that a person continued to live in another place after death, and that the person could take his or her possessions to that place. In fact, most of the jewelry from ancient Mesopotamia was discovered in graves.

In the early 1900s, teams of archaeologists excavated hundreds of tombs at the Royal Cemetery of Ur. They found the tomb of Queen

LEFT: Queen Pu-Abi as she was found in her tomb. In addition to the ornate jewelry she wore in her burial tomb, her ladies-in-waiting also wore jewelry and hair ribbons. Five armed men and four grooms with a wooden sledge drawn by oxen were also buried with the queen.

Pu-Abi, who had been buried with thirteen ladies-in-waiting (attendants). They were believed to have drunk poison in order to accompany their queen to the afterlife. Among the jewelry found, the headdress of Queen Pu-Abi was the most extravagant, finely crafted with gold and precious gems. As Sir Leonard Woolley described it:

> The hair ribbon was a narrow gold or silver strip fixed by a short silver pin, the ends coiled into a small loop for the pin. A wreath consisted of a double string of beads, carnelian rings and short cylinders of lapis lazuli from which hung pendants . . . the most common type of pendant was in the form of gold or sometimes silver "beech" leaves followed by gold or silver plain rings, groups of three long willow-shaped leaves or discs of gold with lapis centres. Gold rosettes were sometimes attached to the wreath or fixed as heads to slender silver hairpins.[2]

At another tomb discovered in Nimrud, a warning, carved in stone, places a curse upon anyone who might disturb Queen Yaba's grave or try to steal her jewelry. It warns that the spirit of anyone who attempted to rob her would wander in thirst for eternity.

Headdress of Queen Pu-Abi, re-created

Music and Musical Instruments

The Mesopotamians loved music. Despite their lack of iPods, stereos, and radios, writings about music and dancing in cities, on religious occasions, and during feasts tell us that music played an important part of both religious and daily Mesopotamian life. Musical instruments discovered in the tombs of important people, and images of musicians on plaques, sculptures, and cylinder seals, show pictures of music being played among all classes of people, from shepherds to soldiers, and from rich people feasting to priests and priestesses singing hymns.

Mesopotamians made and used a variety of drums of all sizes (some as large as five feet in diameter), harps, lyres, trumpets, flutes, and pipes. In the ruins of the city of Ur, three harps and nine lyres were found. They are some of the oldest stringed musical instruments, from the third millennium BCE.

Though we don't know for sure how their music sounded, as there were no recordings or music written down in a way that modern people can read it, some discoveries have helped scientists who study music, called musicologists, attempt to figure out what Mesopotamian songs may have sounded like.

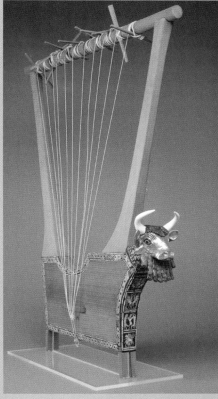

Queen's Lyre from Ur, about 2600–2400 BCE

Clay tablets were found that describe both a musical scale, or group of musical notes, as well as instructions about tuning a lyre. Others have song lyrics and music written on them. Using these two sources of information, the musicologists have played Mesopotamian songs on lyres that were reconstructed and restrung, as much of the instruments had decomposed over time. You can hear some of this music on YouTube at http://uk.youtube.com/watch?v=LvgtAHV4mzw&feature=related and http://www.youtube.com/watch?v=TSWEeBGhz4M.

Cuneiform tablets with songs have also been found among Mesopotamian relics. Both poetry and singing were taught in Sumerian schools, and tablets have been found upon which love songs and religious hymns are written.

The Greeks named the Tigris River after the fierce tiger. The original Sumerian name, Idigna, means "running water" or "swift river." The current of the Tigris is much stronger than that of the Euphrates. Today, Baghdad, the capital city of Iraq, stands on the banks of the Tigris River.

GETTING AROUND IN MESOPOTAMIA

Chapter 5

Though Mesopotamians had the basic things they needed for daily life—grain, meat, fruits, and vegetables for food; clay, soil, and water for building; and animal skins and fabric for clothing—as their civilization grew, people wanted many things to make their daily lives easier and their quality of life better. They began trading grain, fish oil, sesame oil, and textiles to get other things, such as wood, metal, stone, gems, and perfumes. Some items, like gems, were easy for men to carry on foot, with a cart, or on the back of a donkey. Others, like grain, wood, and stone, were heavy and difficult to move over long distances. As their cities were close to the Tigris and Euphrates rivers, it was natural that Mesopotamians developed methods of traveling on water.

WATER TRANSPORTATION

Mesopotamians designed a variety of boats for transporting trade goods to and from cities. They also dug canals for irrigation, which extended water routes to areas that were not directly on the rivers.

Vast numbers of goods were transported via water, including grain, timber, bricks, stone, fruit, oil, animals, and wool. People also used boats to get from one place to another. However, both the Tigris and Euphrates have strong currents and winds that blow north to south. Traveling south via the rivers was easy, but traveling north was nearly impossible. For this reason, some boats were used to carry goods south, then they were taken apart and carried back north over land.

LAND TRANSPORTATION

Travel on land was difficult, as the roads were simply trails worn down by many crossings. By Assyrian times, leaders recognized that good roads allowed armies to travel more quickly and efficiently. As a result, by the 1100s BCE, the Assyrians began to develop land routes, cutting roads through mountains, paving major highways, and building bridges.

It is believed that the chariot was first made in Mesopotamia around 3000 BCE. The Assyrian army was successful partly because it used chariots in warfare, which gave generals an advantage in battle over the opposing army on the ground, as they had a better view from atop the chariot. Chariots were also used during battles to carry messages back and forth quickly.

Besides allowing troops to march easily, these roads were sturdy enough to use with chariots, carts, and wagons. These had wooden wheels and, later, metal bands around the wood to protect the wheels. In places where the land was simply too rocky or too muddy, a vehicle called a sledge, similar to a sled, was used to pull heavy loads. In northern Mesopotamia, roads were better, and both two-wheeled and four-wheeled wagons were used to transport bulky, heavy goods such as lumber from the mountains.

Animals were used to pull land vehicles or to carry loads on their backs. Donkeys and mules were used most often, though horses were introduced for riding about 900 BCE. Camels were also domesticated about 1000 BCE. They could carry much larger loads than donkeys or mules, and they could survive on much less water, making them ideal for travel through the desert.

TRADE

As travel methods improved, so did trade. Some towns and cities grew because they had one particular natural resource, such as a kind of metal, that they could trade for other goods they might need. Marketplaces offered a variety of items, from shells and semiprecious stones like lapis lazuli and obsidian to fine textiles woven in different ways.

Men's trade revolved around metals—silver and gold, as well as copper and tin. Tin was highly desired, as it was used to process copper into bronze, which was used for tools and weapons.

Women manufactured textiles that they sometimes sold through traveling merchants. Women were free to operate their own businesses, and to sell their goods in the marketplace to other women, though only men traveled to other cities to trade. The money women earned was used primarily to support their families. They would buy what they needed for their homes, pay taxes to the king, and purchase more materials for their craft.

Goods were often exchanged in trading colonies or *karums*. One such Assyrian merchant colony was called Karum Kanish, or Kanesh, in Anatolia. Like other *karums*, Kanish was run as a family business. The head of the family lived in the city, while another family member lived at the trading colony. All the money for the business generally came from within the family, but occasionally families would join with a partner. The merchant families decided how the business would be run, but they were required to pay taxes to local rulers. As explained in *Daily Life in Ancient Mesopotamia:*

> Each donkey carried a load of about 90 kilograms of textiles and tin, in addition to loose tin for expenses and taxes on the trip. When the merchants left Asshur, they paid a tax of 1/120 of the value of the goods to the *limmu* official . . . to enter Kanesh, 2/65 of the value was paid to the local ruler. The cities and territories through which the caravans passed also received customs fees and duties at fixed rates.[1]

Goods for trading were often transported by caravan, using donkeys or camels. The large size of the caravans offered some protection against thieves and wild animals.

FYInfo

Mesopotamian Boats

In *The Epic of Gilgamesh*, Utanapishtim (the Mesopotamian version of the biblical Noah) was told by the god Ea:

> The boat which you are to
>   build,
> its dimensions must measure
>   equal to each other:
> Its length must correspond to
>   its width.
> Roof it over . . .[2]

Utanapishtim with his boat

Although no boats remain from Mesopotamian times, clay tablets describe how boats were built. They tell us that boatbuilding was a major industry, and shipyards built large wooden ships for long voyages. While the construction methods are not entirely understood, it is known that these large ships were made by building the outside shell with no interior framework. They were expensive to build, because they were made of wood, which was scarce. People would often hire a ship when they needed one, rather than buy one.

Several types of boats of different sizes and shapes were used in Mesopotamia. Larger boats included barges and ferries that were steered with oars or a pole and pushed south by the current. To go north, they were attached to ropes and pulled by people walking along the riverbank. While these boats were useful for carrying large loads, few were available. Smaller boats were more like today's rubber rafts. They were simply made from an inflated sheep- or goatskin, and one person could lie on it and paddle with his hands and feet. A slightly more elaborate boat, called a *quffa* (or *quppu*), was made from animal skins stretched over a basketlike frame. Two to four men could sit in the *quffa* and row it with oars. Rafts, or *keleks*, were able to carry larger loads. A *kelek* consisted of several inflatable animal skins that were tied together and covered with a platform of reeds. When the animal skins were inflated, the *kelek* sailed efficiently. When the *kelek* reached its southern destination, it could be easily taken apart and deflated, then carried back north on a donkey.

Modern children celebrate the ancient holiday of Akitu, the Assyrian-Babylonian New Year festival. Akitu festivities include parades, bazaars, exhibits of Assyrian art and culture, and traditional Assyrian and Babylonian dance, music, and clothing.

CELEBRATING MESOPOTAMIAN STYLE

Chapter 6

Mesopotamian towns and cities had local gods and goddesses to whom the citizens prayed. They would ask for such things as a plentiful growing season and harvest, protection from natural disasters and personal sufferings such as illness and death, and good luck in general.

Holy days throughout the year honored the local deities. Within every temple was a statue of the local god or goddess, which was seen by the people as the actual deity, not just a piece of stone. On holidays, the statue of the god was taken from its usual place in the temple, paraded around the city, and carried in a procession to visit sacred places outside the city or to visit other gods and goddesses.

The most important festival of the year for Mesopotamians throughout the country was the New Year, or Akitu, festival. The new year began in the spring, on the first days of the month Nisannu. This was the beginning of the growing season, when the seeds were planted.

In the city of Babylon, the Akitu festival was held once a year, at the spring equinox. Some places, however, including the cities of Ur and Uruk, had two celebrations each year, one at the time of sowing the seeds, and a second in the fall, at the time of harvest. In most cases, the festival at the time of planting seeds was the bigger and more important one, lasting eleven or twelve days, while the harvest festival lasted for five days.

The festival was held at two locations. One was the Esagila, or temple of Marduk, in Babylon. The second was a place outside the city, called the Akitu House. During the early days of the Akitu festival, prayer and ritual took place in the temple, which ordinary people did not attend. The head priest would rise two hours before dawn and cleanse himself with water from the river. He would then dress in a linen robe, and begin prayers to Marduk and the other gods to bless the Esagila and the city. The mood of the temple as well as the city was one of sorrow and fear, for it was unknown what lay in the year ahead, and if the city would be blessed by the gods.

Prayers and hymns reflected this mood. As is recorded on ancient cylinders from Lagash, they prayed:

Marduk

> Have pity upon thy city, Babylon
> Turn thy face towards Esagila, thy temple
> Give freedom to them that dwell in Babylon, thy wards![1]

On the fourth day, the high priest would tell the creation myth. Since the new year symbolized a new beginning, in some ways it was similar to the beginning of time.

On the seventh or eighth day of Akitu, the celebration emerged from within the temple. The Mesopotamians believed the king was the embodiment of the gods. He bathed and dressed the statue of the god, and then brought the statue from the temple. A procession led by the king, with the statue, began. There were music, singing, and dancing, and incense was

burned. People kneeled down as the procession went by. The procession eventually arrived at a special place outside the city, called the Akitu House, where a great three-day banquet was held.

On the eleventh day, the procession returned to the city. There was more celebration and festivities, for when the statue was returned to the city, the god's power was renewed and the coming year would be a good one.

GAMES AND RECREATION

Mesopotamians also enjoyed sports and games. Only men participated in sports, which included hunting, wrestling, and boxing, but men and women would watch the games.

Clay pull toy

Large-game hunting was a favorite sport of Assyrian kings, who hunted elephants, bulls, ostriches, and lions. Though the kings often traveled to Syria to hunt the animals on the plains, sometimes the animals were captured and brought back to game reserves. The hunt would be staged as a public event in a fenced-off hunting ground, which was guarded by soldiers with dogs.

A lion that was brought back for public sport was teased to make it angry. Dogs attacked it, and people called beaters hit it with sticks. The king would then hunt and kill the lion on foot, from horseback, or from his chariot. This was a popular form of entertainment for the people of the city, and showed them that their king was strong and fierce. It was believed that a king who was a successful hunter was favored by the gods. King Tiglath-pileser I declared:

. . . with my strong bow, iron arrowheads and sharp arrows, I slew four extraordinarily strong and virile bull elephants in the desert. I killed ten strong bull elephants in the land of Harran (in Syria) and four live elephants I captured. I brought the hides and tusks with the live elephants to my city Ashur.[2]

The Royal Game of Ur was a board game found by archaeologist Sir Leonard Woolley in the Royal Cemetery of Ur. The rules of the game as it was played in Mesopotamian times are unknown, but historians believe it involved trying to get one's pieces to the end of the board. It may be related to the game of backgammon.

Archaeologists have uncovered clay plaques that show men wrestling and boxing. There is also a game mentioned in *The Epic of Gilgamesh* that sounds similar to polo. Rather than playing from horseback, one man rode on the shoulders of another.

As far as quieter games are concerned, board games have been found that were made of stone or clay, with various playing pieces and dice made from bone, clay, stone, or glass. Two games that historians have pieced together are twenty squares, in which the simple board was sometimes scratched into a clay brick; and 58 holes, which is similar to the modern card game called cribbage. It uses a similar board to the one in cribbage, with holes in it for scoring.

Many of the toys found by archaeologists are remarkably similar to toys that children still enjoy playing with today. Dolls, animal figures, and miniature furniture were probably used by Mesopotamian children the same way they are used today. Children also played with small vehicles such as chariots, ships, and wagons, as well as toy weapons, like bows and arrows, slingshots, and boomerangs. Ancient Mesopotamian children played outdoors with jump ropes, balls, and hoops.

Moon Festival

Besides the major annual New Year ritual and celebration, each town or city-state had smaller rituals each month. These were held to ask the gods for help, and prevent the gods from becoming angry and causing misfortune, such as droughts or floods. The Mesopotamians had a lunar calendar, based on the phases of the moon, which had special meaning for them.

The Mesopotamians believed that the moon died at the end of every month—what we now call the new moon, when the moon is in Earth's shadow. On the day of the new moon each month, Mesopotamians believed that the moon descended to the underworld, and then it was reborn.

The day of the new moon, known as The Day of Lying Down, was a holy day. Offerings were made to the moon god, Nanna, also known as Sin. On this day, Nanna visited the underworld in order to meet with other gods. When Nanna's work was completed, he rose, and the moon began to grow, becoming visible again.

Though Mesopotamian astronomers were able to predict eclipses of the moon, people did not understand what was happening, and they were frightened by them. Lunar eclipses were considered an evil omen, and people believed something tragic would happen to their king. In order to stop the bad event, a substitute king, usually a poor man, was chosen. The substitute king was then killed, which the people believed would assure that the real king would remain unharmed.

Worshiping the moon, from a cylinder seal c.2100 BCE

CUNEIFORM WRITING ON A CLAY TABLET

What you need
Self-hardening clay
Stick (a thin branch or chopstick with a pointed
    end works well—a pencil can also be used)
Paper plate
Cuneiform letter chart

What you do
1. Take a piece of clay about the size of a baseball; shape and flatten it onto the paper plate until it is square and about one inch thick.
2. Decide what you want to write. It can be your name, a message, or anything else you want. Using your stick and the cuneiform letter chart, create your tablet.
3. Let your tablet dry overnight.
4. Let someone in your family or a friend use the cuneiform chart to try to read your tablet.

A Cuneiform "Alphabet"

A		N	
B		O	
C		P	
D		Q	
E		R	
F		S	
G		T	
H		U	
I		V	
J		W	
K		X	
L		Y	
M		Z	

BCE

5000   Agricultural, or farming, communities develop in the land that lies between the Tigris and the Euphrates rivers in Asia.

c.4000   In the area of southern Mesopotamia called Sumer, the first cities develop. Its inhabitants are called Sumerians. Uruk, the earliest known city, has 50,000 to 150,000 people.

3200   The oldest known clay tablets with pictograms—the first writing—are made in Sumer.

3000   First Sumerian Dynasty of Ur begins. Under its first ruler, Mesanepada, Ur becomes the capital of and one of the most prosperous city-states in Sumer.

2750   Gilgamesh rules Uruk; Agga rules Kish.

2334–2279   Sargon I rules Mesopotamia, taking over Sumer and Akkad, and uniting the Akkadian Empire. Sargon makes his daughter, Enheduanna, high priestess of the moon god Nanna. She helps unite the empire by merging worship of local deities into worship of goddess Inanna. She is also the first author to sign her name to her work.

2250   Enheduanna dies.

2193   Akkadian Empire begins to collapse as city-states gain independence.

2100   Third Sumerian Dynasty of Ur begins; Sumer and Akkad are reunited; ziggurats are built.

c.2000   Tales from *The Epic of Gilgamesh* are first written down. The first toilets and sewers carry waste away from households.

2000–1740   During the Old Assyrian Period, the Assyrian language is written. Assyrian trading colonies, including Kanish, are established in Anatolia to trade textiles and tin for gold and silver.

1900   First Dynasty of Babylon is established, beginning the Old Babylonian Period. Literary activity flourishes. Though Akkadian is the main language, scribes compose and write works in both the Sumerian and Akkadian languages. Kings communicate with one another through letters.

c.1792   Hammurabi, a great military leader, becomes king of Babylon.

c.1000   Camels are domesticated, and horses are used for riding.

884	Ashurnasirpal II comes to power. He installs Assyrian governors to rule the lands he conquers, which helps to create a centralized state.
721–705	Sargon the Great rules Assyria. In his palace are plumbed toilets.
704–681	King Sennacherib reigns over Assyria.
701	Sennacherib lays siege on Jerusalem, but the siege fails.
689	Sennacherib destroys Babylon.
668	King Ashurbanipal, the last great Assyrian king, begins his rule. He will establish the first library in the Middle East, at Nineveh.
639	Ashurbanipal takes over Babylon.
626	The Neo-Babylonian Period begins with the reign of Nabopolassar, a Babylonian soldier.
612	Babylonians under Nabopolassar conquer Assyrian capital of Nineveh.
604	After the death of his father, Nabopolassar, Nebuchadnezzar II becomes king of Babylon.
597	Babylon captured Jerusalem.
586	Nebuchadnezzar destroys Jerusalem; he deports Jewish prisoners of war to Babylon.
562	Nebuchadnezzar dies. He is succeeded by a line of ineffectual rulers.
539	Babylon falls; Mesopotamia becomes part of the Persian Empire.
CE	
1849	Austen Henry Layard discovers the Library of Ashurbanipal at Nineveh.
1901	French archaeologists lead by Jacques de Morgan discover The Law Code of Hammurabi Diorite stela.
1922–1934	British archaeologist Sir Leonard Woolley finds the tomb of Queen Pu-Abi, along with some 1,800 other graves, at the Royal Cemetery of Ur.

CHAPTER NOTES

Introduction. Kammani Goes to the Doctor
1. Robert Silverberg, *The Dawn of Medicine* (New York: G.P. Putnam's Sons, 1966), p. 97.

Chapter 1. From Democracy to Dynasty
1. Samuel Noah Kramer, *History Begins at Sumer: Thirty-Nine Firsts in Recorded History* (Philadelphia: University of Pennsylvania Press, 1981), p.33.
2. *The Code of Hammurabi,* translated by L. W. King. The Avalon Project; Ancient, Medieval and Renaissance Documents, http://avalon.law.yale.edu/subject_menus/hammenu.asp
3. Ibid.

Chapter 2. Home Between the Rivers
1. Karen Rhea Nemet-Nejat, *Daily Life in Ancient Mesopotamia* (Westport, CT: Greenwood Press, 1998), p. 111.
2. Jean Bottero, *Everyday Life in Ancient Mesopotamia* (Baltimore, MD: The Johns Hopkins University Press, 1992), p. 55.

Chapter 3. The First Writers
1. Samuel Noah Kramer, *History Begins at Sumer: Thirty-Nine Firsts in Recorded History* (Philadelphia: University of Pennsylvania Press, 1981), p. 11.
2. Maureen Gallery Kovacs (translator). *The Epic of Gilgamesh* (Stanford, CA: Stanford University Press. 1989), p. 6.
3. Ibid., p. 9.
4. William Hallo and J.J.A. van Dijk, *The Exaltation of Inanna* (New Haven: Yale University Press, 1968).

Chapter 4. Form and Function
1. Leonard Woolley, *The Art of the Middle East Including Persia, Mesopotamia and Palestine* (New York: Crown Publishers, 1961), p. 60.
2. K.R. Maxwell-Hyslop, *Western Asiatic Jewellery, c. 3600-621 B.C.* (London: Methuen Young Books, 1971), pp. 3–5.

Chapter 5. Getting Around in Mesopotamia
1. Karen Rhea Nemet-Nejat, *Daily Life in Ancient Mesopotamia* (Westport, CT: Greenwood Press, 1998), p. 280.
2. Maureen Gallery Kovacs (translator), *The Epic of Gilgamesh* (Stanford, CA: Stanford University Press. 1989), p. 97.

Chapter 6. Celebrating Mesopotamian Style
1. Henri Frankfort and Samuel Noah Kramer, *Kingship and the Gods: A Study of Ancient Near Eastern Religion as the Integration of Society and Nature* (Chicago: University of Chicago Press, 1978), p. 319.
2. Allison Karmel Thomason, *Luxury and Legitimation: Royal Collecting in Mesopotamia* (Burlington, VT: Ashgate, 2005), p. 188.

FURTHER READING

Books for Young Readers

Bryant, Tamera. *The Life and Times of Hammurabi.* Hockessin, DE: Mitchell Lane Publishers, 2005.

Faiella, Graham. *The Technology of Mesopotamia.* New York: Rosen Publishing Group, 2006.

Farndon, John. *Mesopotamia.* New York: Dorling Kindersley: 2007.

Frankfort, Henri, and Samuel Noah Kramer. *Kingship and the Gods: A Study of Ancient Near Eastern Religion as the Integration of Society and Nature.* Chicago: University of Chicago Press, 1978.

McCaughrean, Geraldine. *The Epic of Gilgamesh.* Grand Rapids, MI: Eerdmans Books for Young Readers, 2003.

Mehta-Johnes, Shilpa. *Life in Ancient Mesopotamia.* New York: Crabtree Publishing, 2004.

Nardo, Don. *Science, Technology and Warfare in Ancient Mesopotamia.* Detroit: Lucent Books, 2008.

Schomp, Virginia. *Ancient Mesopotamia: Sumerians, Babylonians, Assyrians.* New York: Scholastic, 2004.

Woods, Michael, and Mary B. Woods. *Ancient Construction: From Tents to Towers.* Breckenridge, CO: Twenty-First Century Books, 2001.

Works Consulted

Barber, Elizabeth Wayland. *Women's Work: The First 20,000 Years. Women, Cloth and Society in Early Times.* New York: W.W. Norton & Company, 1994.

Bertman, Stephen. *Handbook to Life in Ancient Mesopotamia.* New York: Facts on File, Inc., 2003.

Black, Jeremy A., Anthony Green, Tessa Rickards. *Gods, Demons and Symbols of Ancient Mesopotamia: An Illustrated Dictionary.* Austin, TX: University of Texas Press, 1992.

Bottero, Jean. *Everyday Life in Ancient Mesopotamia.* Baltimore, MD: The Johns Hopkins University Press, 1992.

The Code of Hammurabi, translated by L. W. King. The Avalon Project: Ancient, Medieval and Renaissance Documents http://avalon.law.yale.edu/subject_menus/hammenu.asp

The Electronic Text Corpus of Sumerian Literature http://etcsl.orinst.ox.ac.uk/#

Grayson, Albert Kirk. *Assyrian Rulers of the Early First Millennium B.C.: II (858-745 BC) Royal Inscriptions of Mesopotamia: Assyrian Periods. Vols 1 and 2.* Toronto: University of Toronto Press, 1991.

Hawkes, Jacquetta. *The First Great Civilizations: Life in Mesopotamia, The Indus Valley and Egypt.* New York: Alfred A. Knopf, 1973.

Kramer, Samuel Noah. *History Begins at Sumer: Thirty-Nine Firsts in Recorded History.* Philadelphia: University of Pennsylvania Press, 1981.

McIntosh, Jane. *Ancient Mesopotamia: New Perspectives.* Santa Barbara, CA: ABC-CLIO, 2005.

Maxwell-Hyslop, K.R. *Western Asiatic Jewellery, C.3600-621 B.C.* London: Methuen Young Books, 1971.

Nemet-Nejat, Karen Rhea. *Daily Life in Ancient Mesopotamia.* Westport, CT: Greenwood Press, 1998.

Oriental Institute of the University of Chicago: Ancient Mesopotamia—This History, Our History
http://mesopotamia.lib.uchicago.edu/mesopotamialife/index.php

Penn Museum: Treasures from the Royal Tombs of Ur
http://www.museum.upenn.edu/new/exhibits/ur/index.shtml

Pollock, Susan. *Ancient Mesopotamia.* Cambridge, UK: Cambridge University Press, 1999.

Silverberg, Robert. *The Dawn of Medicine.* New York: G.P. Putnam's Sons, 1966.

Thomason, Allison Karmel. *Luxury and Legitimation: Royal Collecting in Mesopotamia.* Burlington, VT: Ashgate, 2005.

Woolley, Leonard. *The Art of the Middle East Including Persia, Mesopotamia and Palestine.* New York: Crown Publishers, 1961.

On the Internet

The British Museum: Mesopotamia
http://www.mesopotamia.co.uk/menu.html

King Hammurabi and His Code
http://www.historyforkids.org/learn/westasia/history/hammurabi.htm

Metropolitan Museum of Art: Art of the First Cities
http://www.metmuseum.org/explore/First_Cities/firstcities_splash.htm

"Write Like a Babylonian"
http://www.upennmuseum.com/cuneiform.cgi

GLOSSARY

abscess (AB-sess)—A collection of pus in the tissues of the body, often accompanied by swelling.

Akkadian (uh-KAY-dee-un)—People from Akkad, a city in northern Babylonia.

Amorite (AH-muh-ryt)—A member of one of several ancient groups of people living in Babylonia.

Annuna (ah-NOO-nuh)—The "Fifty Great Gods" of Mesopotamia; the children of An.

anoint (uh-NOYNT)—To rub or sprinkle on; to apply an ointment, or oily liquid, to.

aqueduct (AH-kweh-dukt)—A pipe or channel designed to transport water from a remote source, usually by gravity.

Assyrian (uh-SEE-ree-un)—Someone who lived in Assyria, a region in Mesopotamia.

Babylonian (bah-buh-LOH-nee-un)—Someone from Babylon, a city in Mesopotamia.

city-state—A city and its surrounding area with one central government.

congress (KONG-gres)—A formal meeting or assembly of representatives for the discussion, arrangement, or promotion of some matter of common interest.

cultivate (KUL-tih-vayt)—To prepare the ground for raising crops.

cuneiform (kyoo-NEE-uh-form)—Writing that uses wedge-shaped characters.

domesticate (doh-MES-tih-kayt)—To tame an animal to live closely with human beings as a pet or to do work.

dynasty (DY-nuh-stee)—A series of rulers from the same family, or group.

epic (EH-pik)—A long poem, usually centered upon a hero, in which great events are told.

millennium (mih-LEH-nee-um)—A period of one thousand years. *Millennia* is more than one millennium.

ore—A rock from which metal can be extracted.

plaster (PLAH-ster)—A pasty mixture applied to the body for a healing purpose.

shrine—An alter, temple, or some other sacred place dedicated to a god or goddess.

Sumerian (soo-MAYR-ee-un)—Someone or something from Sumer, an area of southern Mesopotamia.

tablet—A flat slab or surface, especially one with engravings.

whitewash (WYT-wash)—A mixture, such as of lime and water, used for whitening walls.

ABOUT THE AUTHOR

Elizabeth Scholl is a teacher and writer of educational materials for students and teachers. She has written numerous books and magazine articles on a variety of social studies and science topics.

Elizabeth has explored the world of ancient Mesopotamia with her students, including the art, literature, mathematics and cultures of the Fertile Crescent. Her students created jewelry, constructed ziggurats, and made cylinder seals and used cuneiform writing, based on their study of Mesopotamia.

In her spare time, Elizabeth enjoys learning about history by visiting museums, traveling and reading. She lives in northern New Jersey with her husband and children.